"It seems only right that a book bearing this ti[...] of one whose life and ministry exemplify such [...] challenging, resounding cry to the rest of us to keep on!"

Alistair Begg, Senior Pastor, Parkside Church, Chagrin Falls, Ohio

"Accurate and honest, direct and encouraging, clear and plain, MacArthur has produced a portrait in words. As Paul reflects Christ, so should the faithful minister. Unintentionally, MacArthur here has written his own autobiography."

Mark Dever, Pastor, Capitol Hill Baptist Church, Washington, DC; President, 9Marks

"*Remaining Faithful in Ministry* is simultaneously as bracing as a cold shower in the early morning and as thrilling as the prospect of a glorious day of adventure. If it doesn't make you want to be a more faithful servant of Christ, beware."

Sinclair B. Ferguson, Chancellor's Professor of Systematic Theology, Reformed Theological Seminary; Teaching Fellow, Ligonier Ministries

"Here is an invaluable reminder of the essential truths necessary for long-term endurance in gospel ministry."

Steven J. Lawson, President, OnePassion Ministries; Professor of Preaching, The Master's Seminary; Teaching Fellow, Ligonier Ministries

"John MacArthur helps us to see from the ministry of the apostle Paul that in the tempests of ministerial life, there is nothing more crucial than an anchor embedded in solid rock."

Conrad Mbewe, Pastor, Kabwata Baptist Church; Chancellor, African Christian University, Lusaka, Zambia; author, *Pastoral Preaching*

"This is a treasure of wisdom for pastors and a book that will encourage all true ministers of the gospel. Every pastor—and future pastor—should read this book, and every faithful minister will treasure it."

R. Albert Mohler Jr., President, The Southern Baptist Theological Seminary

"John MacArthur's insight brought from Scripture in these pages provides a message we continue to need this side of heaven."

Iain H. Murray, author, *Jonathan Edwards: A New Biography* and *Evangelical Holiness*; Founding Trustee, Banner of Truth Trust

"This book is biblically solid, well written, easy to read, deep, engaging, inspiring, brief, and built on the faithful legacy of the apostle Paul. If you begin to read it, you won't stop until you are finished."

Miguel Núñez, Senior Pastor, International Baptist Church, Santo Domingo, Dominican Republic; Founding President, Wisdom & Integrity Ministries

"For elders, seminary students, and pastors of all ages, this is a book for those men who are biblically qualified to shepherd the flock of God and proclaim the Word of God in season and out of season for the glory of God alone."

Burk Parsons, Senior Pastor, St. Andrew's Chapel, Sanford, Florida; Editor, *Tabletalk* magazine

"Here is surprising, countercultural, Pauline wisdom every pastor should heed if he is to endure and flourish."

Michael Reeves, President and Professor of Theology, Union School of Theology

"John MacArthur's half-century of ministry at Grace Community Church in itself provides sufficient warrant to title his latest book *Remaining Faithful in Ministry*. It is a clarion call for pastors to remain faithful to the very end, from one whose life has exemplified faithful ministry."

Derek W. H. Thomas, Senior Minister, First Presbyterian Church, Columbia, South Carolina; Chancellor's Professor of Systematic and Pastoral Theology, Reformed Theological Seminary; author, *Strength for the Weary*

"In these pages, Christ's minister will find genuine courage and strength from the Scriptures that he might fulfill God's calling without wavering. There is more biblical truth in this little book than in most volumes ten times its size."

Paul David Washer, Director, HeartCry Missionary Society; author, Recovering the Gospel series; *Knowing the Living God*; *Discovering the Glorious Gospel*; and *Discerning the Plight of Man*

Remaining Faithful
in Ministry

Other Crossway books by John MacArthur

Ashamed of the Gospel: When the Church Becomes Like the World, third edition (2009)

Biblical Doctrine: A Systematic Summary of Bible Truth (coeditor, 2017)

Fool's Gold?: Discerning Truth in an Age of Error (editor, 2005)

The Freedom and Power of Forgiveness (2009)

The Glory of Heaven: The Truth about Heaven, Angels, and Eternal Life, second edition (2013)

The Gospel according to God: Rediscovering the Most Remarkable Chapter in the Old Testament (2018)

The Inerrant Word: Biblical, Historical, Theological, and Pastoral Perspectives (editor, 2016)

The Scripture Cannot Be Broken: Twentieth Century Writings on the Doctrine of Inerrancy (editor, 2015)

Think Biblically!: Recovering a Christian Worldview (editor, 2009)

Truth Endures: Landmark Sermons from Forty Years of Unleashing God's Truth One Verse at a Time (2011)

Remaining Faithful
in Ministry

9 Essential Convictions for Every Pastor

John MacArthur

WHEATON, ILLINOIS

Library of Congress Cataloging-in-Publication Data

Names: MacArthur, John, 1939- author.
Title: Remaining faithful in ministry : 9 essential convictions for every pastor / John MacArthur.
Description: Wheaton, Illinois : Crossway, 2019. | Includes bibliographical references and index.
Identifiers: LCCN 2018033422 (print) | LCCN 2018051954 (ebook) | ISBN 9781433563041 (pdf) | ISBN 9781433563058 (mobi) | ISBN 9781433563065 (epub) | ISBN 9781433563034 (tp) | ISBN 9781433563065 (ePub) | ISBN 9781433563058 (Mobipocket)
Subjects: LCSH: Pastoral theology. | Perseverance (Ethics)—Biblical teaching. | Paul, the Apostle, Saint.
Classification: LCC BV4011.3 (ebook) | LCC BV4011.3 .M28 2019 (print) | DDC 253—dc23
LC record available at https://lccn.loc.gov/2018033422

LB		29	28	27	26	25	24	23	22	21	20	19
15	14	13	12	11	10	9	8	7	6	5	4	3	2	1

Contents

FIFTY YEARS OF
FAITHFULNESS

The
work
of the
Word

2 TIMOTHY 4 : 2

Introduction

Four successive generations of my immediate ancestors included men who faithfully served the Lord as pastors. Two of them (my father and grandfather) were still alive and engaged in full-time ministry when I came along, and their steadfast devotion to serving Christ made a lasting impact on me.

My grandfather died of cancer while I was still a young boy. I remember vividly that before he became too sick to preach, he had prepared a sermon titled "Heavenly Records." His one regret as he lay on his deathbed was that he wasn't going to have an opportunity to preach that last sermon. My dad had copies of the manuscript printed and distributed them at the funeral. So my grandfather preached a sermon on heaven *from* heaven.

My father served the Lord faithfully until he died at the age of ninety-one. I watched and learned from him over the years—literally a lifetime of faithful ministry—and he passed on to me a rich legacy of dedicated ministry. His influence on me is immeasurable.

When I enrolled in seminary as a young man, my dad introduced me to Dr. Charles Lee Feinberg, who at the time was the world's leading evangelical authority on Hebrew, Jewish history, and Old Testament studies. Dr. Feinberg grew up as an Orthodox

Jew and was trained to be a rabbi before he was converted to Christ. He had a PhD in archaeology and Semitic languages. He loved the Scriptures, and he took a particular interest in me. His instruction and encouragement were invaluable to me throughout those years in seminary.

So I was richly blessed with a number of close, highly qualified mentors who helped prepare me for ministry. I'm indebted to all of them and deeply grateful for everything they taught me.

But when people ask who has been my greatest influence and model for pastoral ministry, I have to say hands down it is the apostle Paul. During my earliest years in ministry I was captivated by the power of his example. I've always seen myself as a kind of latter-day version of Timothy, trying my best (though often frustrated by my own failures) to learn from and emulate Paul—especially his courage, his faithfulness, his deep love for Christ, and his willingness to stand alone.

Of all the words Paul ever left under the inspiration of the Holy Spirit for us to consider, the text that has left the most indelible impression on my heart is 2 Timothy 4:6–8, the apostle's last recorded declaration of faith before giving his life for the gospel's sake. Just after encouraging Timothy with the words "fulfill your ministry" (v. 5), he writes:

> For I am already being poured out as a drink offering, and the time of my departure has come. I have fought the good fight, I have finished the race, I have kept the faith. Henceforth there is laid up for me the crown of righteousness, which the Lord, the righteous judge, will award to me on that day, and not only to me but also to all who have loved his appearing.

To come to the very end of life and be able to say all those things with such confident assurance is all too rare. In Paul's case, it is especially striking. It's an exultation rather than an elegy. But it comes from the pen of an apostle whose utter disdain for boasting was well known. Paul's steadfast refusal to exalt himself is evident throughout his epistles. So this final declaration of triumph must be read as an expression of deep gratitude, settled peace, and sweet relief.

No wonder. Perhaps no other minister has ever faced as many hardships, as much opposition, or such relentless suffering as the apostle Paul. Yet he followed Christ with unwavering faithfulness to the very end. Here's how he summarized his ministerial experiences. He says he served the Lord

> with far greater labors, far more imprisonments, with countless beatings, and often near death. Five times I received at the hands of the Jews the forty lashes less one. Three times I was beaten with rods. Once I was stoned. Three times I was shipwrecked; a night and a day I was adrift at sea; on frequent journeys, in danger from rivers, danger from robbers, danger from my own people, danger from Gentiles, danger in the city, danger in the wilderness, danger at sea, danger from false brothers; in toil and hardship, through many a sleepless night, in hunger and thirst, often without food, in cold and exposure. And, apart from other things, there is the daily pressure on me of my anxiety for all the churches. (2 Cor. 11:23–28)

Despite all those hardships, Paul was still devoted to Christ when he drew his final breath. Amazingly, when he "finished the race," there were no earthly crowds to celebrate his triumph. No one gave him a trophy. No one hailed him or his achievements.

Notice, also, that as he began writing his last recorded words, his second epistle to Timothy, Paul didn't sound triumphant at all. From a human viewpoint there is a pervasive loneliness in that closing chapter of the apostle's final epistle. The thankless world was about to chop off his head. His life was about to end in ignominious fashion. This tireless man who wrote a significant portion of the New Testament had also planted more than a dozen strategic churches and trained countless other pastors, evangelists, and missionaries. He had personally taken the gospel to multitudes across the Mediterranean region—from Jerusalem and Antioch to Rome. But he was now going to die virtually all alone. To all earthly appearances, this was a tragic ending to a disappointing life.

But Paul himself had a better, more heavenly, perspective. He was neither frustrated nor disillusioned. Just before giving his life for the gospel, the apostle wrote this one final inspired epistle to Timothy, the protégé to whom he would hand the baton. The tone of his instruction and counsel suggests that as Paul's death drew near, his spiritual son Timothy may have been totally discouraged—perhaps even on the brink of bailing out of the ministry.

Paul faces facts squarely, without fear or regret. He does not downplay or try to gloss over the fact that many of his former fellow laborers and disciples had already forsaken him, and even those who were spiritually aligned with him were keeping their distance. He practically began that final epistle to Timothy by writing, "You are aware that all who are in Asia turned away from me" (2 Tim. 1:15). Then in his final chapter, he added these details:

Demas, in love with this present world, has deserted me and gone to Thessalonica. Crescens has gone to Galatia, Titus to Dalmatia. Luke alone is with me. Get Mark and bring him with you, for he is very useful to me for ministry. Tychicus I have sent to Ephesus. When you come, bring the cloak that I left with Carpus at Troas, also the books, and above all the parchments. Alexander the coppersmith did me great harm; the Lord will repay him according to his deeds. Beware of him yourself, for he strongly opposed our message. At my first defense no one came to stand by me, but all deserted me. May it not be charged against them! (4:10–16)

What amazes me is that Paul was neither stymied nor embittered by all the adversity. In fact, he saw his circumstances as an occasion to give God glory. His very next words were: "But the Lord stood by me and strengthened me, so that through me the message might be fully proclaimed and all the Gentiles might hear it. So I was rescued from the lion's mouth. The Lord will rescue me from every evil deed and bring me safely into his heavenly kingdom. To him be the glory forever and ever. Amen" (vv. 17–18).

Thus Paul remained faithful to the end. He persevered out of sheer love for the Lord, for the simple joy of obedience, with his hopes fixed firmly on heaven.

That attitude is the key essential for anyone seeking to be a faithful minister of Christ. Paul said, "Be imitators of me, as I am of Christ" (1 Cor. 11:1; cf. 4:16). It is a mandate that has hung over my heart and conscience for all the years I have been in ministry.

A question I have long pondered is, How does someone do that? How can a person go through every ministerial setback Paul experienced and remain steadfast, immovable, always abounding in the work of the Lord? How can we cultivate that same kind of commitment? How can we finish the race triumphantly when our course is filled with seemingly insurmountable obstacles— "afflict[ions] at every turn—fighting without and fear within," as Paul himself describes it (2 Cor. 7:5)?

Detailed answers to those questions are outlined by the apostle himself in 2 Corinthians 4. That is the primary chapter I want to explore in this booklet.

The Background of 2 Corinthians

The apostle Paul wrote his second inspired epistle to the Corinthians during a period in his ministry when he had every reason to be discouraged. He had founded the church in Corinth and served as pastor there for eighteen months (Acts 18:11). His missionary work necessitated his moving on, but he kept in close contact with the Corinthians. His first inspired epistle to that church is a long, detailed breakdown of several problems that were troubling the church. It is an exhausting array of very difficult pastoral challenges, but Paul answers each issue with fatherly kindness, rich wisdom, and simple clarity. Through it all, he shows a deep and genuine concern for the Corinthians. He is patient, helpful, encouraging—the epitome of a kind-hearted shepherd who genuinely knew and loved the sheep.

By the time Paul wrote 2 Corinthians, however, he was under severe attack in Corinth by some peddlers of false doctrine— phony apostles—who had arrived on the scene in Paul's absence and infiltrated the Corinthian church. The false teachers were doing their best to destroy Paul's reputation. They were aggressively trying to undermine his influence in that church. Because the teaching of these men was a corruption of the gospel, it posed a serious threat to the spiritual health and testimony of the Corinthian church. The false apostles had focused their attack on Paul personally. Both his character as well as the content of his teaching were under relentless assault. So he was forced to defend himself. He does so in an interesting way—never boasting of his own accomplishments or otherwise trying to elevate himself, but by exalting Christ in a way that exposed the hypocrisy and self-serving falsehoods of the false teachers.

The gist and the focal point of Paul's self-defense is summarized in 2 Corinthians 4:5: "What we proclaim is not ourselves, but Jesus Christ as Lord, with ourselves as your servants for Jesus' sake." That is a succinct statement of every true minister's calling and commission. The gospel is a message about Christ, and at all times he is to be the singular focus of the message we proclaim. False apostles and hirelings always seem to find a way to shift attention to themselves. They make themselves the central character of every anecdote. They paint themselves as the hero of every story they tell. Thus they make their preaching little more than a display of their own egos. Pulpits today are full of men who constantly preach themselves.

No one—least of all the Corinthians—could legitimately accuse the apostle Paul of doing that. Here's how he described his ministry in Corinth: "I decided to know nothing among you except Jesus Christ and him crucified" (1 Cor. 2:2). Even when the audience demanded something else, or something more, Paul preached Christ. "For Jews demand signs and Greeks seek wisdom, but we preach Christ crucified" (1:22–23). In Galatians 6:14 he said, "Far be it from me to boast except in the cross of our Lord Jesus Christ." That was his perspective.

I think when he wrote, "What we proclaim is not ourselves," Paul probably had in mind words from the Old Testament prophecy of Jeremiah about prophets who spoke out of their own imaginations: "Thus says the LORD of hosts: 'Do not listen to the words of the prophets who prophesy to you, filling you with vain hopes. They speak visions of their own minds, not from the mouth of the LORD'" (Jer. 23:16). As Jesus said in John 7:18, "The one who speaks on his own authority seeks his own glory." Paul was definitely not seeking his own glory. Instead, he says, "We proclaim . . . Jesus Christ as Lord, *with ourselves as your servants for Jesus' sake*" (2 Cor. 4:5).

The word "servants" somewhat tones down the force of Paul's statement. He's not describing himself as a butler dressed in expensive finery or a waiter at a classy restaurant. The word he uses means "slaves"—human chattel; someone who is legally the property of someone else. He's acknowledging that he has been bought with a price, and he is no longer his own (cf. 1 Cor. 6:19–20). That conviction was the starting point of Paul's entire ministry philosophy.

As he unpacks his philosophy in 2 Corinthians 4, Paul gives us a detailed answer to the question of how he remained faithful in the midst of so much adversity. He begins the chapter with this triumphant declaration: "Therefore, having this ministry by the mercy of God, we do not lose heart" (v. 1).

Notice, first, that phrase at the end of the verse: "we do not lose heart." Verse 16 repeats the exact same words. So the brief testimony Paul gives in this chapter is bracketed with identical statements about his determination to serve Christ without "los[ing] heart."

English translations tend to understate what Paul was saying. The King James Version says, "We faint not." Modern translations typically say, "We don't give up" (or some close equivalent). The Greek verb Paul uses *(egkakeō)* is a combination of two common words. The first is a form of the preposition *en,* which speaks of being at a state of rest or surrender "in" or "among" something. The main root is a noun, *kakeō,* meaning "wickedness" or "depravity." So the sense of the expression is, "We do not give in to evil"—much stronger than if he were merely saying, "We don't grow weary."

In other words, this is not only about resisting fatigue, discouragement, or cowardice. There's a powerful note of holy defiance in Paul's tone. What he means is, "We don't defect; we refuse to give in to evil in any way."

What prompts him to say that in this context? In a subtle way, he is acknowledging by implication that his experience with the Corinthians had the potential to drive him to abandon the ministry. That problem-ridden church had caused him such deep difficulty and penetrating disappointment that a lesser person might have been tempted to throw in the towel. The Corinthians' sins, their shallowness, their rebellion, and their fickleness toward Paul are all plainly evident in the two inspired epistles he wrote to them. There was moral impurity in that church, jealousies, lawsuits, incest, and shameful desecration of the Lord's Table. On top of all that, their criticism of him was heartbreaking, and he tells them that (12:11–14).

In 1 Corinthians 16:12 Paul says he urged Apollos to take a team of qualified leaders to Corinth to try to resolve the problems there. But the Corinthian church was so fraught with trouble that

Apollos had no desire to return there. In short, this was a church no one wanted to pastor.

Paul actually wrote them at least four letters. Two are recorded in the New Testament, and the other two (not part of the inspired canon) are mentioned in the two we have. From the content of the letters, it is evident that whatever was remedied by Paul's admonitions in 1 Corinthians fell short of the mark, because the church so quickly opened up to these theological mischief makers who had an agenda to destroy the church's confidence in Paul. These self-appointed false apostles relentlessly accused and maligned the true apostle.

Paul paid a visit to Corinth that did not go well. He went away feeling worse than before he arrived. At that point he wrote a severe letter to them. Also, in the wake of that disastrous visit, he resolved not to go back to Corinth again (2 Cor. 2:1).

But when it became clear that these dangerous false teachers were gaining a dominant influence in the church, Paul's heart was broken. It was the kind of thing that could make a minister abandon the ministry. They were blasting his character. They were questioning his credentials. Perhaps they were exploiting his controversy with Peter (see Gal. 2:11). They were slandering him in every way possible. They said he was unimpressive as a speaker. They made this charge as personally insulting as possible, saying he was not only unskilled as an orator (2 Cor. 11:6), but his personal presence was contemptible as well (10:10). It was a depressing experience to work with that church.

Paul barely concealed his own frustration with the Corinthian church throughout this second epistle. You see it from the very start in the emphasis he gives to God's mercy and comfort: "Blessed be the God and Father of our Lord Jesus Christ, the

Father of mercies and God of all comfort, who comforts us in all our affliction" (1:3–4). In chapter 2 he talks about pain. It is the pain of sorrow—his own pain in the aftermath of that disastrous visit to Corinth, and the Corinthians' pain when they received his severe letter. Chapters 4, 6, 7, 10, 11, 12, and 13 all address problems in that assembly, especially their sour, cynical attitude toward the self-sacrificial apostle who had founded that church and to whom they owed everything. Here is a man who is dealing with an obdurate and supremely disappointing congregation of people into whose lives he had poured his own life and energy. So when he lists all his hardships in 11:23–27 and punctuates it by saying, "Apart from [these] other things, there is the daily pressure on me of my anxiety for all the churches" (v. 28), that statement is loaded with significance.

Yet in spite of all the antagonism, calamity, and deprivation he faced throughout every phase of his ministry, Paul did not give in to evil. Despite the problems he had to deal with in every church he planted, all the opposition he encountered, all the discouragements that assaulted him, all the suffering he endured, he nevertheless remained loyal and true to Christ in every respect. Of all the characters we meet in Scripture, other than Christ himself, Paul best embodies indefatigable faith, unflagging persistence, and steadfast determination. There is no more dramatic biblical example of pure devotion to Christ. In 2 Corinthians 4 the apostle himself explains the factors that contributed to this remarkable perseverance.

Here are nine reasons Paul did not lose heart. *One*, he saw himself as a steward of God, entrusted with a new and better covenant. *Two*, he saw that role as not only a high privilege but also a great mercy extended to him by the grace of God. *Three*, he was determined to keep his own heart pure and upright, and he understood that faithfulness is a key element in the pursuit of true integrity. *Four*, he had one controlling passion—namely, his devotion to preaching the Word of God. *Five*, he understood that God's Word never returns void (Isa. 55:11), so he was not stymied by man-made standards of success or failure. *Six*, he was a humble man, not looking for accolades or recognition, but pursuing God's glory at all costs. *Seven*, he knew that God uses our suffering as a means of sanctifying us, and he was eager to be a partaker in the fellowship of Christ's sufferings. *Eight*, he was familiar with the great heroes of faith in the Old Testament, and he sought to emulate their courage. And *nine*, he had his heart fixed on heaven and things above, knowing full well that the sufferings of this present time are not worthy to be compared with such glory.

Those are nine unwavering convictions that kept Paul faithful. You'll see them clearly as we work our way through the text of 2 Corinthians 4. Buckle in, and we'll take some time to examine each one of those ideas in closer detail.

1

Convinced of the Superiority
of the New Covenant

Second Corinthians 4 begins with Paul saying, "Therefore, having this ministry . . ." (v. 1). The word "therefore" of course points us back to the previous chapter. It may sound like an old bromide, but this is an important rule to follow: when you see the word *therefore* in Scripture, you have to ask what it's *there for*. In this case, it ties what Paul is about to say to the topic he was dealing with in chapter 3. That chapter is a detailed comparison and contrast of the old and new covenants.

The inauguration of the new covenant (signaling the termination of the old covenant) was not a trifling shift that Paul observed with academic interest as an outsider. It was a sea change that completely upended his life plan and shattered his worldview. Paul was a Hebrew of the Hebrews from a line of Pharisees who belonged to the noblest of the twelve Jewish tribes. He was raised from birth to be zealous for the law. He was devoted to the Pharisaical tradition. He was so fastidious with regard to the law's ceremonies and external features that he looked absolutely blameless to anyone who observed his life. That is the substance of his personal testimony in Philippians 3:4–6. (He gave a similar testimony to King Agrippa in Acts 26:4–5, speaking about the fastidiousness of his legalism and his strict adherence to the demands of the old covenant.)

But when Paul was struck down on the Damascus Road by the Lord Jesus himself, everything changed. The story of his conversion (a version that features the pertinent historical details) is told in Acts 9, and Luke further records how Paul himself retold the story twice more, in Acts 22:3–21 and 26:12–23. Paul's testimony in Philippians 3 skips the historical details in order to stress the far-reaching spiritual implications of his rebirth. There he states in graphic language how profoundly his thinking and his lifestyle were changed at his conversion. He says, in essence, that when Christ arrested him that day, Paul suddenly realized that all his old-covenant legalism was no more valuable to him and no less offensive to God than if he tried to offer a pile of manure on the altar. Paul was awakened to the truth of Isaiah 64:6:

> We have all become like one who is unclean,
>   and all our righteous deeds are like a polluted garment.

The Hebrew noun Isaiah used speaks of a scrap of fabric that has been soiled and stained with an unclean bodily discharge. It is fit for nothing but burning. This is purposely repulsive imagery, but it shows how God views all attempts by sinners to earn righteousness under the law.

What Paul further learned is that a truly perfect, spotless righteousness—the perfect obedience demanded by the law—is imputed to those who believe in Christ. During his earthly life Christ fulfilled every demand of the old-covenant law and more (Matt. 3:15). And he did it all on behalf of his people, "so that in him we might become the righteousness of God" (2 Cor. 5:21). Therefore, Paul says he discarded his own hard-won self-righteousness because it was no better than human sewage. *I count those things as dung,* he said, "in order that I may gain Christ and be found in him, not having a righteousness of my own that comes from the law, but that which comes through faith in Christ, the righteousness from God that depends on faith" (Phil. 3:8–9).

When Paul was converted, every facet of his life changed dramatically, starting with his attachment to the Mosaic covenant. Paul saw instantly that the law condemns sin and cannot save sinners (Rom. 3:20; 7:9–11; Gal. 3:10). "The law brings wrath" (Rom. 4:15). And the law passes the death sentence on everyone without exception, because no one can keep the law. The law therefore has power only to kill sinners, not to redeem them.

The point is not that the law itself is evil. On the contrary, "the law is holy, and the commandment is holy and righteous and good" (Rom. 7:12). Without the law, we would have a deficient understanding of what God's righteousness requires of us (v. 7). The problem lies with the sinner, not with the law.

But the new covenant supplies and perfects everything that was lacking in the old covenant. In the words of Hebrews 8:6, "Christ has obtained a ministry that is as much more excellent than the old as the covenant he mediates is better, since it is enacted on better promises." More than that, the new covenant completely supersedes and does away with the old: "In speaking of a new covenant, he makes the first one obsolete" (v. 13).

The old covenant was spelled out in hundreds of detailed and demanding commandments; the new covenant is centered on

Christ and his finished work. If the centerpiece of the old covenant was the law of Moses (with its rigorous ceremonial demands and its inflexible sentence of death), the heart and soul of the new covenant is the promise of life in Christ. Obviously, the new covenant is "a better covenant" (Heb. 7:22).

The old covenant could not provide righteousness. Christ provides for his people the righteousness the law demanded but could never supply. The old covenant was temporary; it "was being brought to an end" (2 Cor. 3:7). But the new covenant is permanent, never to be replaced. The old covenant pronounced death and doom on sinners; the new covenant offers life.

"The letter kills, but the Spirit gives life" (2 Cor. 3:6). That's the key point Paul makes in 2 Corinthians 3, and he stresses every one of those contrasts. In verse 7 he calls the old covenant "the ministry of death" and the new covenant "the ministry of the Spirit." Verse 9 speaks of the old covenant as "the ministry of condemnation" and the new covenant as "the ministry of righteousness." In verse 11 he contrasts "what was being brought to an end" (the old covenant) with "what is permanent" (the new covenant). That same idea is echoed in Hebrews 13:20, which speaks of the new covenant as "the eternal covenant."

To sum up, the old covenant offered sinners no hope. The new covenant offers "such a hope [that] we are very bold" (2 Cor. 3:12). The ideas of boldness, confidence, sufficiency, and competence constitute a thread that ties chapter 3 together (vv. 4–6, 12). Paul is giving us his answer to a question he had raised at the end of chapter 2: "Who is sufficient for these things?" His answer, in a single sentence, is, "Not that we are sufficient in ourselves to claim anything as coming from us, but *our sufficiency is from God*" (3:5). And this entire discussion of the new covenant in 2 Corinthians 3 is therefore a detailed account of how the distinctive features of the new covenant have made the apostles and their fellow laborers competent for the ministry God appointed them to. Every point Paul makes in this context applies to everyone in the history of the church who has faithfully preached the gospel, down to and including those whom God has ordained and called into ministry in our generation and in the years to come.

The old covenant was cloudy and veiled (vv. 13–14); the new covenant is clear and unshrouded. All the mysteries of the old covenant are revealed in Christ. That's what Paul means in verse 14 when he says the veil of the old covenant is removed in Christ. Hebrews 1:1–2 likewise states that God's final and sufficient revelation for this age has been given to us once and for all in Christ. That text and its cross references constitute a formal declaration of the finality and eternality of the new covenant.

It is significant that Paul refers to the new covenant as "the ministry of the Spirit" (2 Cor. 3:8). The coming of the Holy Spirit at Pentecost is one of the key events that signaled the transition from the old to the new covenant. The Spirit was of course at work throughout the Old Testament era as well, but the full depth of Trinitarian doctrine is simply not prominent in the Old Testament. The Spirit's place and function in the triune Godhead is one of the monumental truths from which the old covenant veil has been removed. He also seems to have a new and unique role under the new covenant, permanently indwelling and empowering every believer, steadily conforming them to the image of Christ by moving them from one level of glory to the next (vv. 17–18). This of course is one of the anchors that held Paul in the knowledge that his competency for the task of ministry came from God. It was proof that the Lord himself would supply sufficient grace for every need. The indwelling Spirit of God assured Paul that even the extreme trials and disappointments he would face in his ministry would ultimately only perfect, confirm, strengthen, and establish him (cf. 1 Pet. 5:10). "The Spirit helps us in our weakness" (Rom. 8:26). That, as a matter of fact, is the whole theme and substance of Romans 8.

Here was a man who came out of the hopelessness of the old covenant into the certainty and security of the new covenant. Paul never lost his sense of wonder when he thought of the new covenant. He knew what he had been delivered from. Every trial he ever faced was dwarfed by the deliverance that had already been provided to him by God's sovereign grace through Jesus Christ. It was a staggering, unmerited honor for him to be called into the Lord's service, and he more than anyone understood that.

Paul clearly had that very thing in mind when he originally raised the question of his own adequacy. He wrote:

> But thanks be to God, who always leads us in triumph in Christ, and manifests through us the sweet aroma of the knowledge of Him in every place. For we are a fragrance of Christ to God among those who are being saved and among those who are perishing; to the one an aroma from death to death, to the other an aroma from life to life. And who is adequate for these things? (2 Cor. 2:14–16 NASB)

Indeed, no human in himself could ever take on himself such a weighty responsibility or have that kind of everlasting impact. But Paul is a preacher of the new covenant, an instrument of God who will make an impact on people's eternity, either in heaven or in hell. What fool who is given such a calling would settle for anything less than that?

This is a powerful argument for staying focused on gospel truth—proclaiming the whole message of the gospel, studying the details of the gospel, defending the doctrines of the gospel, meditating on the promises of the gospel, encouraging one another with the precepts of the gospel, and singing about the glories of the gospel. We must never forget what a privilege it is to be called as ministers of the new covenant. That is the first and foundational key to Paul's unflagging perseverance.

2

Convinced That
Ministry Is a Mercy

Paul's deeply rooted understanding that his calling was a totally undeserved expression of God's great mercy to him was itself one of the core convictions that kept him faithful to the end. He was called and commissioned for ministry solely "by the mercy of God" (2 Cor. 4:1). That is of course true of every person who is called to serve Christ in ministry. It's not a privilege we have earned. God doesn't call us because of any aptitude or proficiency we develop on our own. We are not in ministry because we are somehow more righteous or more worthy than others. It is a mercy. We all know our own hearts well enough that we should never have confidence in our own flesh. We feel our weakness. We are regularly plagued with personal failings. And I'm sure all genuine believers might wonder why the Lord called us, why he continues to keep us in his fold. For Paul in particular, it was mind-boggling to think that Christ, whom he had once fiercely persecuted, would show him such mercy—even making this former Pharisee an apostle.

Listen to Paul's own words:

> I thank him who has given me strength, Christ Jesus our Lord, because he judged me faithful, appointing me to his service, though formerly I was a blasphemer, persecutor, and insolent opponent. But I received mercy because I had acted ignorantly in unbelief, and the grace of our Lord overflowed for me with the faith and love that are in Christ Jesus. The saying is trustworthy and deserving of full acceptance, that Christ Jesus came into the world to save sinners, of whom I am the foremost. But I received mercy for this reason, that in me, as the foremost, Jesus Christ might display his perfect patience as an example to those who were to believe in him for eternal life. (1 Tim. 1:12–16)

Every good thing that comes to us is an undeserved mercy. By God's great mercy he calls us, equips us, and surrounds us with men and women who come alongside to serve the Lord in partnership with us. It's an undeserved privilege, and the moment any minister begins to see his calling any other way, he is on the road to disaster.

In his old life as a Pharisee, Paul would never have described himself as the foremost of sinners. Consider again the testimony he gives in Philippians 3. Bear in mind in that context, the apostle was refuting some false teachers who insisted that Gentile converts could not be justified—counted righteous before God—unless they were first circumcised. In other words, they made circumcision the necessary instrument of justification, rather than faith in Christ alone. Paul refers to them as "dogs . . . evildoers . . . those who mutilate the flesh" (Phil. 3:2). They were apparently the same cult of gospel twisters who were troubling the Galatian churches, and who seemed to target Paul wherever he went. These heretics gained a following by boasting about the rigorous way they observed the fine points of Jewish ceremonial law, so Paul answered them by recounting his own apostolic credentials: "If anyone else thinks he has reason for confidence in the flesh, I have more: circumcised on the eighth day, of the people of Israel, of the tribe of Benjamin, a Hebrew of Hebrews; as to the law, a Pharisee; as to zeal, a persecutor of the church; as to righteousness under the law, blameless" (vv. 4–6).

He was recounting how he thought of himself as a Pharisee, not describing his perspective as an apostle. Prior to his encounter with Christ on the Damascus road, Paul thought of himself as "blameless"—and indeed, he had mastered the art of external piety. But the law demands Godlike perfection (Matt. 5:48), and even the great Saul of Tarsus, applying all his energies and a lifetime of Pharisaical training and discipline, fell far short. Once his eyes were opened to the reality of his sin, he abandoned every reason he ever thought he had for boasting. He counted it all as "rubbish" (Phil. 3:8). The Greek noun is *skubalon*, which means "dung." The very things he had once been most inclined to boast about were emblems of the most shameful self-righteousness—and reminders of the wicked arrogance that had driven him to murderous zeal against the people of God. He truly saw himself as the lowest of sinners, and the least deserving of divine mercy. He wrote, "I am the least of the apostles, unworthy to be called an apostle, because I persecuted the church of God" (1 Cor. 15:9).

Deep gratitude for God's mercy therefore remained at the forefront of Paul's thoughts for the remainder of his ministry, and it often surfaced in his epistles. When he wrote to the church at

Rome, he acknowledged the great debt he owed to God's mercy, "because of the grace given me by God to be a minister of Christ Jesus to the Gentiles in the priestly service of the gospel of God" (Rom. 15:15–16). Almost every time he mentioned his own calling, he spoke of it as "the grace of God given to me" (Rom. 12:3; 1 Cor. 3:10; 15:10; Gal. 1:15; 2:9).

To the Ephesians, he wrote:

> I was made a minister according to the gift of God's grace, which was given me by the working of his power. To me, though I am the very least of all the saints, this grace was given, to preach to the Gentiles the unsearchable riches of Christ, and to bring to light for everyone what is the plan of the mystery hidden for ages in God who created all things, so that through the church the manifold wisdom of God might now be made known to the rulers and authorities in the heavenly places. (Eph. 3:7–10)

Paul fully intended to take the gospel to the very top rung of earthly authority, right into the court of Caesar (Acts 28:19). Beyond that, as he says here, he wanted the manifold wisdom of God to be made known as publicly as possible, to the open shame of every demonic principality and power. Paul knew full well that goal would cost him dearly in terms of suffering and persecution. When friends in Caesarea begged him not to go to Jerusalem because his freedom (not to mention his life) was at stake, he replied, "I am ready not only to be imprisoned but even to die in Jerusalem for the name of the Lord Jesus" (Acts 21:13). Like the apostles spoken of in Acts 5:41, he rejoiced that he was counted worthy to suffer dishonor for the name of Christ.

What gave him the ability to maintain that attitude was his keen awareness that to be in the ministry at all was a glorious mercy he did not deserve. It's why even when he was under attack, rather than lash out at his accusers or trumpet his own accomplishments and abilities, he always simply acknowledged the mercy of God in calling him into ministry in the first place.

Convinced of the Need
for a Pure Heart

A third unshakable conviction that drove Paul to remain faithful was the knowledge that he needed to maintain a holy life, even in secret. The Pharisees were masters of imposture (Matt. 23:25–28), harboring sins of the heart while carefully maintaining a pious exterior. Before his conversion, Saul of Tarsus was surely no exception. As a believer, however, he categorically repudiated every hint of hypocrisy. He wrote, "We have renounced disgraceful, underhanded ways" (2 Cor. 4:2).

His adversaries in Corinth had evidently accused him of wearing a righteous facade to cover a secret life of sin. Indeed, reading between the lines in 2 Corinthians, they had apparently gone so far as to suggest that he was using his position as an apostle to take unfair and immoral advantage of women. In 10:2, for example, he mentions "some who suspect us of walking according to the flesh," and says he was "count[ing] on" showing such people how bold he could be in a face-to-face encounter when he finally had an opportunity to confront them and answer the slander and innuendo they had spread in their deliberate, sinister attempts to impugn his moral character.

Determined to defame Paul, these false apostles had also accused him of being motivated by greed and love of money. They implied that he was a boastful man, exaggerating his accomplishments. Of course they offered no proof with any of those charges. No proof existed; the charges were all utterly and demonstrably false. But rather than outline a lengthy defense against such frivolous accusations, Paul simply stated the moral standard that lay at the foundation of his entire ministry philosophy: *We have renounced every secret thing that might cause shame. My life is an open book.*

Was Paul perfect? No. At the same stage of his ministry when he wrote this epistle to the Corinthians, he wrote to the church at Rome and said, "When I want to do right, evil lies close at hand. . . . Wretched man that I am! Who will deliver me from this body of death?" (Rom. 7:21, 24). Though he had renounced hypocrisy, he remained deeply aware of his own wretched fallenness. There's not a hint of contradiction there. In fact, the statement in Romans 7 affirms the claim of 2 Corinthians 4. He acknowledges his wretchedness; he doesn't try to hide it. He's more than willing to confess it. That's as far from hypocrisy as any former Pharisee has ever gone.

The tense of the Greek verb translated "renounced" in 2 Corinthians 4:2 is *gnomic aorist*, signifying a generic truth without limiting the action to past, present, or future. Here, it speaks of a permanent, persistent, continuous, and habitual action. It's not a one-time past tense, as if Paul were saying, "I once did that." His renunciation of hypocrisy and underhandedness is a constant, settled, ongoing commitment. When he entered his new life with

Christ, he *permanently* abandoned not only the doctrine but also the duplicity of Pharisaism.

This is actually an echo of something Paul said at the very start of this epistle. Because his adversaries had accused him of being a braggart, he wrote, "Our boast is this, the testimony of our conscience, that we behaved in the world with simplicity and godly sincerity, not by earthly wisdom but by the grace of God, and supremely so toward you" (1:12). It wasn't a fleshly boast at all (as if he were bragging about his own knowledge, skill, or accomplishments). Whatever virtue he could point to was not attributable to "earthly wisdom" or human strength. Paul's sanctification was entirely "by the grace of God," and that's where he expressly gives credit.

But it intrigues me that what he pointed to in answer to false accusations was the testimony of his own conscience. *You can denounce me all you want; I have a clear conscience. You're accusing me; but my conscience is not. That doesn't mean I'm perfect (O wretched man that I am), but it does mean that I don't hold onto sin. I don't cultivate an inner life of secret shame. I have a clear conscience.*

That is the value of keeping a pure heart. It doesn't matter what comes at you; if your conscience is clear, no accusation sticks. The conscience is a gift from God. It's like a skylight or window, not a lamp. In and of itself, it's not a source of light, but when kept clear and illuminated by the light of God's Word, the conscience lets in that light—even in a world of darkness. Conscience is an invaluable tool for revealing our true motives. A clear and biblically informed conscience will either accuse or excuse us, depending on whether we are guilty or innocent.

How do you keep your conscience clear? By winning the sin battle on the inside. When Paul says, "We behaved in the world with simplicity and godly sincerity," he is describing a life of transparent holiness. That requires the mortification of sin on the inside, starting with evil thoughts and desires. Jesus stressed this truth repeatedly: "Out of the heart come evil thoughts, murder, adultery, sexual immorality, theft, false witness, slander. These are what defile a person" (Matt. 15:19–20). A well-informed, healthy conscience serves as a warning signal to alert to the rise of evil thoughts.

Charles Wesley wrote a wonderful hymn that is a prayer to God for a sound and effective conscience:

> I want a principle within
> Of watchful, godly fear,
> A sensibility of sin,
> A pain to feel it near.
> Help me the first approach to feel
> Of pride or wrong desire;
> To catch the wandering of my will,
> And quench the kindling fire.
>
> From thee that I no more may stray,
> No more thy goodness grieve,
> Grant me the filial awe, I pray,
> The tender conscience give.
> Quick as the apple of an eye,
> O God, my conscience make!
> Awake my soul when sin is nigh,
> And keep it still awake.
>
> Almighty God of truth and love,
> To me thy pow'r impart;
> The burden from my soul remove,

The hardness from my heart.
O may the least omission pain
My reawakened soul,
And drive me to that grace again,
Which makes the wounded whole.[1]

Paul knew that in order to have a pure life, he had to keep a clear conscience—and that meant he had to deal with the first hint of sin in his mind and heart. If we don't do that, when evil desire conceives, it gives birth to sin, and when sin is fully grown, the result is death (James 1:15).

---

1. Charles Wesley, "I Want a Principle Within," 1749.

Convinced of the Need to Preach the Word Faithfully

Another principle that kept Paul from bailing out of the ministry was the knowledge that he had a solemn duty before his Master to preach the Word of God accurately and persistently, without altering it or watering it down. He says, "We refuse to practice cunning or to tamper with God's word, but by the open statement of the truth we would commend ourselves to everyone's conscience in the sight of God" (2 Cor. 4:2).

The word "cunning" translates the Greek word *panourgia*. The King James Version renders it "craftiness," and various modern translations say "trickery," "deceit," or "deception." The Greek term includes all those nuances. There is no obvious English synonym that has all the same connotations. It's derived from the words *pas* ("all") and *ergon* ("work"), implying a willingness to do anything and everything to serve one's own ends. It denotes someone who is artful, devious, conniving, and shrewd. This is a pragmatist who is willing to do absolutely anything to gain whatever end is desired. *Panourgia* sounds similar to *kakourgia,* a word that speaks of criminality, lawbreaking, or any kind of deliberate wrongdoing. There's a similarly negative flavor to the word *panourgia* wherever it is used, and no wonder. The idea that the end justifies the means inevitably breeds unprincipled conduct and unsavory character.

Just a couple of chapters before this, Paul wrote, "We are not, like so many, peddlers of God's word" (2:17). The word used for "peddlers" is derived from the Greek word *kapēlos,* meaning "huckster." Paul essentially says, *I'm not playing a shell game with divine truth. I'm not watering it down. I'm not cheapening it. I'm not a street hawker making merchandise of the gospel.*

In 4:2 when Paul says, "We refuse to . . . tamper with God's word," he uses a word for "tamper" that means "to ensnare." The word is derived from a word meaning "decoy." The word was sometimes used of shady wine merchants who duped people into buying diluted wine. What Paul means, then, is that he doesn't employ any kind of ruse to lure unsuspecting souls into his circle of influence. He doesn't entice people by beguiling them with phony promises, diluted doctrines, twisted Bible texts, or other deceitful devices.

What Paul says here is clean contrary to the prevailing philosophy of ministry in many large, influential churches today. In our generation it seems there's a glut of pragmatic ministry philosophies and utilitarian people in high-profile positions of church leadership. They will do anything to draw a crowd, and they assiduously avoid "the open statement of the truth." They make no appeal to the human conscience. They downplay or (more often) totally ignore essential gospel truths. Their influence has had a detrimental effect on the spiritual health of the broad evangelical movement.

Paul was making it absolutely clear (in answer to what his critics were saying behind his back) that he had renounced every hint of religious chicanery. Con men and charlatans have always been attracted to religion because there are lots of people in the world who confuse gullibility with faith. Innocent but credulous people are particularly susceptible to spiritual subterfuge, and false teachers who are greedy for gain see them as easy marks. No doubt in his Pharisee days, before his conversion to Christ, Paul was once somewhat willing "to practice cunning or to tamper with God's word." One of the things Jesus condemned the Pharisees for was the adroitness with which they adjusted Scripture to fit their own preferences: "You have a fine way of rejecting the commandment of God in order to establish your tradition!" he said in Mark 7:9.

As an apostle, Paul would have none of that. He had renounced everything disgraceful, underhanded, or crafty. Instead, he says, "by the open statement of the truth we would commend ourselves to everyone's conscience in the sight of God."

"Open statement of the truth"—that refers to the candid, unabridged, fearless proclamation of the whole counsel of God. That is tragically a rare commodity in the church of the twenty-first century. Paul sees it as the only approach to ministry that has any real integrity. Religious mountebanks manipulate the Scripture to make it sound more appealing. They tamper with it to make it say something they only wish it said. They tone it down to make it more palatable. They twist it to try to make its truth sound more in step with the values and beliefs of secular culture. They play with it as if it were a toy. There are some extremely popular preachers today who do *all* those things. But in the end, they defeat the very purpose for which the truth exists.

Romans 2:15 indicates that the basic substance of God's moral law is written on every human heart, and the human conscience bears witness to it. That is the only effective point of attachment any gospel preacher has with a sinner. If your goal is to win the sinner's goodwill and admiration by toning down the hard truths of the gospel, you may make a friend, but you will not make a convert.

Paul is saying, *No matter if I face rejection, trials, hardships, difficulties, disagreements, assaults, persecution, even what comes unjustly—criticism, physical attacks, or death—I will be faithful to the truth because I know the truth carries its own validation.* Truth commends itself to the human conscience. We don't have to defend the Word of God. It has a glory all its own. It has a power all its own.

It was Charles Hodge who said, "[Paul] knew that the truth had such a self-evidencing power that even where it was rejected and hated it commended itself to the conscience as true. And those ministers who are humble and sincere, who are not wise in their own conceit, but simply declare the truth as God has revealed it, commend themselves to the consciences of men."[1] That is great news for anyone who proclaims the gospel. We don't have to soften the gospel or alter it in any way. It's not our job to gain converts through any kind of manipulation. As Paul himself says in Romans 1:16, the gospel itself "is the power of God for salvation." That power is manifest not in our comments on the gospel, not in human public-relations strategies, not in the cleverness of the preacher, not in cultural savvy, but in "the open statement of the truth."

We must also remember that we are ministering "in the sight of God," as Paul says at the end of verse 2. God is watching. We cannot shirk our duty to preach his Word faithfully.

---

1. Charles Hodge, *Commentary on the Second Epistle to the Corinthians* (New York: Robert Carter & Bros., 1860), 83.

Convinced That the Results Belong to God

Far too many pastors abandon the Pauline approach to ministry because they conclude in the midst of some trouble or opposition that the approach Paul used "doesn't work." They say things like, "I tried preaching from God's Word without holding anything back—declaring the hard truth of the law followed by the good news of the gospel, trusting God that his Word would find a connection to the sinner. But our church remained small. Meanwhile, there was a megachurch in our town featuring smoke machines, a light show, and topical sermons with lots of references to popular culture. They were drawing thousands every Sunday. So now we're using that approach. We decided to stop trying to do what worked in the first century and get in step with the times. We gave Paul's strategy a try, but it just didn't yield positive results."

Let's remember, first of all, that the response Paul got to his preaching was often violently negative. At Lystra he was stoned and left for dead (Acts 14:19). Paul's original ministry at Ephesus culminated in a citywide riot (Acts 19:23–39). The church in Corinth was riddled with problems. The churches in Asia Minor flirted with abandoning the principle of divine grace (Gal. 5:4).

But Paul understood that the results did not depend on him. Paul said, "I planted, Apollos watered, but God gave the growth" (1 Cor. 3:6). "All Scripture is breathed out by God and profitable for teaching, for reproof, for correction, and for training in righteousness" (2 Tim. 3:16). When declared with conviction and clarity, God's Word is *always* profitable, even when the results are not immediately obvious. In fact, the supreme encouragement for making God's Word the centerpiece of our ministry strategy is summed up in a promise that comes from God's own mouth in Isaiah 55:10–11:

> As the rain and the snow come down from heaven
> and do not return there but water the earth,
> making it bring forth and sprout,
> giving seed to the sower and bread to the eater,
> so shall my word be that goes out from my mouth;
> it shall not return to me empty,
> but it shall accomplish that which I purpose,
> and shall succeed in the thing for which I sent it.

Sometimes God's design is teaching and training in righteousness; sometimes it's rebuke and correction. The gospel is a fragrance from life to life for those who hear and believe. But for the "many" who are intent on traveling the broad road that leads to destruction, the gospel is a fragrance from death to death (2 Cor. 2:15–16). Either way, when we proclaim the truth fully, clearly, and faithfully, we have done our part. The results are up to God. As Paul says in our text, "Even if our gospel is veiled, it is veiled to those who are perishing. In their case the god of this world has blinded the minds of the unbelievers, to keep them from seeing the light of the gospel of the glory of Christ, who is the image of God" (2 Cor. 4:3–4).

It's never right to adjust the message or employ manipulative strategies in order to elicit a more positive response. Doing so suggests that the minister deserves at least partial credit for the results. And be forewarned: the "results" of tampering with the gospel message are always negative, even if the strategy produces a superficially positive response. In our generation, false and truncated "gospels" have filled churches with false converts—people who have never actually felt the weight of their guilt or known what it means to put their trust in Jesus as Lord.

Paul makes a powerful statement about those who respond negatively to the gospel. *If our gospel is veiled,* he says, *there's a reason.* When we witness or preach, we are talking to a category of people identified by Paul as "those who are perishing" (v. 3). He referred to the same category of people in 1 Corinthians 1:18: "The word of the cross is folly to those who are perishing." He is speaking of people who are spiritually dead and spiritually blind by nature (Eph. 2:1–3), and in 2 Corinthians 4:4 he says they are doubly blind because Satan, the god of this world, has blinded their minds. They are profoundly blind. They cannot see "the light of the gospel of the glory of Christ, who is the image of God."

Nothing in all the universe—nothing in the eternal heavens, either—is brighter than the glory of Christ. It is "the glory of God in the face of Jesus Christ" (v. 6). It is blazing light, but unbelievers cannot see it. Spiritually, they are stone dead and therefore utterly blind. That is who we are talking to, every time we proclaim the gospel to unbelievers.

Paul names a second category in 1 Corinthians 1:18: "To us who are being saved [the gospel] is the power of God." He names the same two categories ("those who are being saved and . . . those who are perishing") in 2 Corinthians 2:15. Each individual in all of humanity falls in one or the other of those two categories.

What separates "those who are being saved" from "the unbelievers" (4:4)? Were the elect not also unbelievers, too, before the gospel came to them? Paul dealt thoroughly with that question very clearly at the start of his first epistle to the Corinthians. Just after saying that no human being should ever boast in the presence of God, he says, "Because of him you are in Christ Jesus" (1 Cor. 1:29–30). In other words, God's saving grace is what removes the veil of blindness and enables "those who are being saved" to see the glory of God in the face of Jesus Christ. That is why Paul says, "Let the one who boasts, boast in the Lord" (v. 31). And that is why he says in 2 Corinthians 4:5, "What we proclaim is not ourselves, but Jesus Christ as Lord, with ourselves as your servants for Jesus' sake."

As we noted at the beginning, that verse is the linchpin and a perfect summary of Paul's ministry philosophy. It is the necessary stamp of authenticity you will find on all true ministry.

The immediate context is crucial. Paul was saying that he preached "Jesus Christ as Lord" because people in their natural, fallen state, are utterly blind and hopelessly oblivious. The gospel ("the power of God for salvation") is the only means by which the darkness of spiritual death can be dispelled.

On the one hand we might say that the doctrine of human depravity is the most discouraging doctrine in the Bible. Unbelievers are spiritually dead, without the capacity to love God, obey him, or please him (Rom. 8:7–8)—much less believe in him by their own freewill choice or initiative. But in another sense, as we seek to share the gospel with a hostile world, we should be encouraged by the fact that it is outside the scope of our range or abilities to awaken dead sinners. It means our *only* duty is to be faithful, through the open statement of gospel truth, to appeal to everyone's conscience in the sight of God. God himself will use the gospel to open the eyes and penetrate the hearts of those whom he is saving. If the gospel is truly the only power God uses to save people, then the results of our ministry are not dependent on whatever skill or cleverly devised strategies we might bring to the task.

In other words, the minister who endures to the end, remaining faithful to Christ, must be anchored in the great reality of God's sovereign saving grace. God is the one who awakens sinners from that inert state of spiritual lifelessness (Eph. 2:4–10). Paul says so emphatically in our primary text: "For God, who said, 'Let light shine out of darkness,' has shone in our hearts to give the light of the knowledge of the glory of God in the face of Jesus Christ" (2 Cor. 4:6). The *only* way any unbeliever will ever see the light is when God does a creative miracle to awaken the soul. Just as when he first said, "'Let there be light,' and there was light" (Gen. 1:3), he is able by his word alone to awaken dead sinners to the light of his glory.

Our task, again, is simply to proclaim the Word faithfully. God will use it to accomplish his good pleasure. If I thought someone's eternal destiny hinged on my skill as a preacher, I think I would stay mute. The weight of that kind of responsibility would be unbearable. Nor do I wish to get any credit when God uses the preached Word to convert a soul. I'm happy (like Paul) to acknowledge that all glory for the salvation of souls belongs to God, because I could never minister in the way God has called me to serve if I thought the results depended on my skill or cleverness.

Paul remained faithful to the very end because he knew that the results of his ministry were entirely up to our sovereign God. Otherwise, the way his life and ministry ended might have provoked extreme discouragement or even despair.

6

Convinced of His Own Insignificance

Alongside Paul's confidence in God's sovereignty, he was kept faithful by a powerful conviction that he himself was nothing (1 Cor. 3:7; 2 Cor. 12:11). Paul did not have an exalted view of himself. He spoke of himself as the foremost of sinners (1 Tim. 1:15); "the least of the apostles, unworthy to be called an apostle" (1 Cor. 15:9); and "the very least of all the saints" (Eph. 3:8). Here in 2 Corinthians he writes, "We have this treasure in jars of clay, to show that the surpassing power belongs to God and not to us" (4:7).

Paul pictures himself as a cheap container holding a priceless treasure. What is the treasure? It is "the knowledge of the glory of God in the face of Jesus Christ" (v. 6). That's a reference to the gospel. Paul was entrusted with it and called to proclaim it, and he saw it as the treasure of all treasures, far surpassing any other treasure—or all treasures combined. And he viewed himself as a worthless vessel made of dirt. That description, by the way, applies not only to Paul himself but to all of us whom Christ has commissioned to take the gospel into all the world. We are, ultimately, just pottery made from the dust of the earth.

It is a startling contrast: the eternal glory of God in the face of Jesus Christ, revealed to sinners through the gospel, which is carried into all the world by feeble, flawed, fragile, ugly messengers—"jars of clay."

Bear in mind, this is part of Paul's response to his critics in Corinth. They said he was unimpressive. "His bodily presence is weak, and his speech of no account" (10:10). Again we see that he made no attempt to refute charges like those. He conceded the point. He wasn't embarrassed by such criticisms. He likens himself to a cheap pot made of baked clay—breakable, replaceable, ordinary, ugly, with no intrinsic value, whose usefulness is subject entirely to the discretion of its maker and master.

He was not using hyperbole. The imagery is perfectly apt. Like all men, Paul was imperfect—and he never shied away from confessing that. Furthermore, what Paul said of himself is true of all ministers. As A. T. Robertson wrote, "If God could not use poor instruments and feeble voices, He would make no music."[1] Even the best of men are frail and fallible. The heroes of faith listed in Hebrews 11 were all people with feet of clay—or better yet (to stay with Paul's metaphor) they were vessels made entirely of clay.

Clay vessels are useful only because of the skill of the potter who makes them. Left alone, clay would harden into a useless, stonelike clod. The adjective translated "clay" is *ostrakinos*, the

---

1. A. T. Robertson, *The Glory of the Ministry: Paul's Exultation in Preaching* (London: Revell, 1911), 147.

word for terra cotta. He's not describing fine china, but a plain, drab, totally unadorned clay pot.

In 2 Timothy 2:20 Paul says, "In a great house there are not only vessels of gold and silver but also of wood and clay, some for honorable use, some for dishonorable." Clay vessels were the cheapest, most common pieces of household crockery—literally disposable. But they were used for widely varying purposes, some sublime, some ignoble.

In Paul's time, it was not unusual for wealthy people and kings to store their gold and other valuables in simple clay pots. These would then be buried in the ground for safekeeping. But a vessel of this type was actually better suited for a less honorable purpose: to remove the household waste.

Sir Thomas More is regarded by Catholics as a saint. But his language when he talked about Martin Luther was frequently too profane to reproduce here. He called him (among other things) "a lousy little friar, a piece of scurf, a pestilential buffoon, a dishonest liar."[2] But his favorite insult was to compare Luther to a privy pot. Listen to what he said:

> [Luther] has nothing in his mouth but privies, filth and dung, with which he plays the buffoon more foully and impurely than any buffoon, of whom none has ever been found besides this one such a stupid butt of men's scorn that he would cast into his mouth the dung which other men would spit out into a basin. . . . He has devoted himself totally to hell. . . . If he will swallow down his filth and lick up the dung with which he has so foully defiled his tongue and his pen, there will be not lacking those who, as is fitting, will discuss serious matters in a serious way. But if he proceeds to play the buffoon in

---

2. Cited in Peter Ackroyd, *The Life of Thomas More* (London: Anchor, 1998), 226.

the manner in which he has begun, and to rave madly, if he proceeds to rage with calumny, to mouth trifling nonsense, to act like a raging madman, to make sport with buffoonery, and to carry nothing in his mouth but bilge-water, sewers, privies, filth, and dung, then let others do what they will; we will take timely counsel, whether we wish . . . to leave this mad friarlet and privy-minded rascal with his ragings and ravings, with his filth and dung.[3]

Thomas More repeatedly referred to Luther as "Father Tosspot."[4]

In his better moments, Luther (like Paul) would freely concede the point. He was in many ways a deeply flawed man and keenly aware of that fact. As insulting as his adversaries could be, Luther was quite capable of smiting himself with reminders of his unworthiness. He knew very well that he was a vessel made of dirt. He said, "We all belong in the ground; there's no way around it."[5]

In a similar fashion, Isaiah said, "I am a man of unclean lips, and I dwell in the midst of a people of unclean lips" (Isa. 6:5). That in turn is a lament that calls to mind Paul's famous groan, "Wretched man that I am! Who will deliver me from this body of death?" (Rom. 7:24). In 1 Corinthians 4:13 Paul said, "We have become, and are still, like the scum of the world, the refuse of all things." He uses two Greek nouns that speak of filthy scrapings, the muck left in the bottom of a garbage container when it has been emptied. Paul certainly did not have an inflated view of his own significance.

---

3. Thomas More, *The Complete Works of St. Thomas More*, vol. 5, *Responsio ad Lutherum*, ed. John M. Headley, trans. Elizabeth F. Rogers (New Haven, CT: Yale University Press, 1969), 683.

4. Ibid., 315, 317, 351.

5. Martin Luther, *Table Talk*, vol. 54, Luther's Works, ed. Theodore G. Tappert and Helmut T. Lehmann (Philadelphia: Fortress, 1967), 277.

The power of the glorious gospel has nothing to do with us, except that we are the clay pots in which this precious treasure is hid. We are weak. We are common, plain, fragile, breakable, dishonorable. But our weakness does not diminish the power of the gospel. "It is the power of God for salvation" (Rom. 1:16).

Convinced of the Benefit of Suffering

Several verses in the middle of 2 Corinthians 4 are devoted to another powerful conviction that kept Paul faithful—namely, that he knew the benefit of suffering. He was not only a clay pot; he was a brutally battered clay pot who never won any kind of popularity contest:

> We are afflicted in every way, but not crushed; perplexed, but not driven to despair; persecuted, but not forsaken; struck down, but not destroyed; always carrying in the body the death of Jesus, so that the life of Jesus may also be manifested in our bodies. For we who live are always being given over to death for Jesus' sake, so that the life of Jesus also may be manifested in our mortal flesh. So death is at work in us, but life in you. (vv. 8–12)

Four contrasts appear in verses 8 and 9. All of them speak of Paul's determination to persevere: "Afflicted . . . but not crushed.

"Perplexed, but not driven to despair." "Persecuted, but not forsaken." And "struck down, but not destroyed." Verses 10–12 then expound on a fifth contrast: death and life. Through all of this, Paul says to the Corinthians, *The fruit of my suffering is your benefit.*

In chapter 12 Paul thoroughly explains the benefit of his suffering. He first mentions the inestimable privilege he had to be carried into the highest heaven, "whether in the body or out of the body I do not know, God knows" (v. 3). In other words, the experience was so real and so vivid that he didn't know if he was literally transported into heaven, or if it was a vision. Either way, it was an unparalleled experience. But Paul says next to nothing about it. He gives no description of what heaven was like. Instead he says this: "To keep me from becoming conceited because of the surpassing greatness of the revelations, a thorn was given me in the flesh, a messenger of Satan to harass me, to keep me from becoming conceited" (v. 7). Twice (once at the start of the sentence and once at the end) he says this was done to keep him humble.

He uses a word for "thorn" that signifies something larger than a sliver of wood. It is the word you would use to describe a stake or a tent peg. It's not a barb from a rosebush, but more like a sharp stick driven through his flesh. It's a painful wound.

It isn't a literal piece of wood that speared him. This is a metaphor signifying some highly painful and persistent grief or trouble. It is not a mere irritant, but something reminiscent of a stab wound to his soul where the lance that caused the puncture was left in the laceration. He refers to it as a messenger of Satan. So it seems he is describing a person, not a disability or illness. Whoever this person was, he served as an instrument of Satan, tormenting Paul. Quite possibly it was the leading false teacher who spearheaded the assault on Paul's character and reputation in Corinth. Paul prayed three times that the Lord would remove the cause of his pain, but the Lord would not remove it because it kept the great apostle humble. Surely one of the reasons trouble always accompanies ministry is that it's one of the main ways God keeps his ministers humble.

God told Paul, "My grace is sufficient for you, for my power is made perfect in weakness" (v. 9). Our infirmity keeps us dependent on the grace of God, and our weaknesses also magnify God's grace. "Apart from me," Jesus said in John 15:5, "you can do nothing."

What was Paul's response when he learned the thorn would not be taken away? He says, "Therefore I will boast all the more gladly of my weaknesses, so that the power of Christ may rest upon me. For the sake of Christ, then, I am content with weaknesses, insults, hardships, persecutions, and calamities. For when I am weak, then I am strong" (2 Cor. 12:9–10).

Here is a group of false teachers led by a demon-possessed leader tearing up this church that Paul founded and loves. The people in this church are his own spiritual children whom he holds in his heart with the deepest affection. If there's sin in their midst, he feels the pain. If there's trouble in the church, he is always there to help. And he asks the Lord to remove this demonic trial that is causing him persistent pain—but the Lord says, *No. You need to stay humble, and you need to learn that your strength is found in your weakness.*

That whole vignette from chapter 12 sheds light on Paul's remark in 4:10, where he says he is "always carrying in the body the death of Jesus." All the pain, suffering, and even death that came to him stemmed from his adversaries' fiery contempt for Christ. Christ is the one they wanted to make suffer. But he wasn't there, so they inflicted their brutality on the one who represented him.

Although they meant it for evil, God meant it for good. He had a benevolent purpose in Paul's suffering: "so that the life of Jesus may also be manifested in our bodies." Paul reiterates the point in the next verse (4:11): "For we who live are always being given over to death for Jesus' sake, so that the life of Jesus also may be manifested in our mortal flesh." He says it again in verse 12: "So death is at work in us, but life in you." In other words, *This is how it goes: I put my life on the line. I suffer persecution. I am tortured. I am persecuted so that I am weak. And out of my weakness comes spiritual strength that brings life to you.*"

That is why ministers need to embrace suffering. Those who *don't* embrace their suffering are more likely to defect from ministry, fall on the hillside before they get to the summit, or abandon the faith altogether.

Christ, of course, was stalked by his enemies until they killed him. Paul followed the same course, for his Lord's sake. But all the way along, in his weakness, God was working powerfully. The talent, intellect, and skill of the apostle Paul could never be the explanation for the long-range impact of his life's work. By his own confession, he was nothing, a nobody. The whole world held him in contempt. He was feeble, suffering, despised by his adversaries, and abandoned by virtually all his friends. But God used those very weaknesses to demonstrate the power and perfection of divine grace.

8

Convinced of the Need for Courage

Another factor that kept Paul faithful was his determination to serve Christ courageously. Put simply, Paul did not presume that ministry in the service of Christ should or would be easy, so his expectations were never disappointed when the trials came. He was dauntless.

You see Paul's courage in countless ways. In Acts 27, for example, Paul is a prisoner being transported to Rome, where he would be put on trial for his life. Adverse winds push his ship off course and into the teeth of a storm. Ultimately the ship breaks up near the shore of Malta. Throughout the entire ordeal, Paul displays a supernatural sense of calm and a powerful sense of leadership, and in the end, every man on that ship owed his life to Paul's great courage—even though as a prisoner, he was doubtless the lowest ranking individual on that ship. While drying by a fire on the shore, "Paul had gathered a bundle of sticks and put them on the fire, [and] a viper came out because of the heat and fastened on his hand" (Acts 28:3). Paul calmly "shook off the creature into the fire and suffered no harm" (v. 5). That picture of Paul is beautifully symbolic of the courage and determination he showed despite all the hardships he listed in 2 Corinthians 11:23–27. Look at that list once more:

> Labors . . . imprisonments . . . beatings . . . often near death. Five times I received at the hands of the Jews the forty lashes less one. Three times I was beaten with rods. Once I was stoned. Three times I was shipwrecked; a night and a day I was adrift at sea; on frequent journeys, in danger from rivers, danger from robbers, danger from my own people, danger from Gentiles, danger in the city, danger in the wilderness, danger at sea, danger from false brothers; in toil and hardship, through many a sleepless night, in hunger and thirst, often without food, in cold and exposure.

Only one of the three shipwrecks is described for us in Scripture, which means in all likelihood that the numerous trials recorded in the book of Acts are just a small sample of the relentless hardships Paul courageously endured.

The time when Paul was stoned is especially noteworthy. Luke mentions it almost in passing in Acts 14. Paul was ministering in Lystra, and some Jewish militants pursued him there from Iconium and Antioch. They had conspired in a plot to kill Paul because in Iconium he and his missionary team had "entered together into the Jewish synagogue and spoke in such a way that a great number of both Jews and Greeks believed" (Acts 14:1). Paul's tormenters caught up with him in nearby Lystra, "and having persuaded the crowds, they stoned Paul and dragged him out of the city, supposing that he was dead" (v. 19). The very next verse says, "But when the disciples gathered about him, he rose up and entered the city." Notice: he went straight back to Lystra, gathered his things, traveled to the next town, and began preaching again. That's not all. The *next* verse says, "When they had preached the gospel to that city and had made many disciples, they returned to Lystra and to Iconium and to Antioch" (v. 21). In other words, they went right back not only to the town where Paul was stoned, but also to the two localities where the gang of would-be murderers lived.

Returning to Jerusalem after his final missionary journey, Paul stopped along the way in Caesarea. There the prophet Agabus came and prophesied that Paul would be arrested and turned over to Gentile authorities. Paul's response? "I am ready not only to be imprisoned but even to die in Jerusalem for the name of the Lord Jesus" (Acts 21:13). His desire was to stand in the court of Caesar and declare the gospel to the world's most powerful ruler—who was also without a doubt one of the most evil men who ever lived: Nero. Paul knew Nero despised Christians and routinely slaughtered them. He was fully aware that an audience with the emperor would probably cost him his life—and ultimately, it did. On the eve of his martyrdom, he wrote, "I am already being poured out as a drink offering, and the time of my departure has come. I have fought the good fight, I have finished the race, I have kept the faith. Henceforth there is laid up for me the crown of righteousness, which the Lord, the righteous judge, will award to me on that day" (2 Tim. 4:6–8).

Years before, already knowing full well what his devotion to Christ might ultimately cost him, he wrote 2 Corinthians 4:13, declaring that he had "the same spirit of faith according to what has been written." In other words, his confidence was rooted in

Scripture. Because in this context he was highlighting the tension between life and death, he reached back to the prayer of Psalm 116:8–10, where the psalmist writes:

> You have delivered my soul from death,
>> my eyes from tears,
>> my feet from stumbling;
> I will walk before the LORD
>> in the land of the living.

> I believed, even when I spoke,
>> "I am greatly afflicted."

Paul takes a phrase from verse 10 of that psalm as it appears in the Septuagint (the Greek translation of the Old Testament), and he echoes the psalmist's declaration of faith: "I believed, and so I spoke" (2 Cor. 4:13).

I love the simplicity and forthrightness of that. We speak what we believe. Paul is saying, "My convictions give rise to courage. If I truly believe something, I say it. I don't edit myself."

People sometimes ask me whether I think much about how people might react to my preaching, especially when I'm dealing with a topic that might not be in sync with popular opinion or political correctness. The answer is no. I am called to be an ambassador, not an arbiter or a deal broker. I'm tasked with delivering a message, not with masterminding a compromise between human opinion and divine revelation. I have been commissioned to declare God's Word. I need to think like a preacher, not like a diplomat. When I preach, I can think of one thing only: *Is this true?* I believe; therefore I speak.

It is the very essence of faith to say, "I believe, and so I speak." If I truly believe something, I must say it, no matter if it brings persecution. Silence or compromise might mean a measure of comfort, acceptance, or even popularity. But it lacks integrity and smacks of cowardice and infidelity. Like Paul, the Reformers, and every faithful minister who has ever been used by God, we are bound to speak what we believe, no matter the cost. We must have that kind of courage.

Aren't you afraid you might die, Paul?

No.

Why?

Paul explains why in verse 14: "knowing that he who raised the Lord Jesus will raise us also with Jesus and bring us with you into his presence." If we are killed, we will be resurrected. The sting is out of death.

Furthermore, Paul says, "It is all for your sake, so that as grace extends to more and more people it may increase thanksgiving, to the glory of God. So we do not lose heart" (vv. 15–16). *We do not give in, no matter what, trusting that more people will be converted to Christ. They will be added to the eternal hallelujah chorus, giving thanks everlastingly to God's glory.*

Convinced That Future Glory
Is Better Than Anything
This World Could Offer

Although Paul spent several chapters in 2 Corinthians defending his calling and explaining his ministry, his central focus and singular interest from start to finish was the Lord's glory. He wasn't defending himself for his own sake. Concern for his personal reputation would not have been a sufficient motive for Paul to write like this. He hated defending himself, because he disliked anything that smacked of boasting (2 Cor. 10:12–13; 11:16–21; 12:9). But he had to answer his accusers for the gospel's sake and for the honor and glory of the Lord.

He was insistent about this. "What we proclaim is not ourselves, but Jesus Christ as Lord" (2 Cor. 4:5). In a later chapter of this same epistle, Paul quotes from the prophet Jeremiah: "'Let the one who boasts, boast in the Lord.' For it is not the one who commends himself who is approved, but the one whom the

Lord commends" (10:17–18). All glory rightfully belongs to the Lord. "His name alone is exalted; his majesty is above earth and heaven" (Ps. 148:13). No one understood that principle better than the apostle Paul. It was a truth he reiterated again and again: "Whether you eat or drink, or whatever you do, do all to the glory of God" (1 Cor. 10:31).

And the promise of eternal glory meant more to Paul than any earthly comfort. It was the hope that anchored him through all life's difficulties—and that's obvious in this passage. Glory was the theme at the end of 2 Corinthians 3, and he returns to it at the end of chapter 4. Paul knew the glory of eternity would more than compensate for whatever troubles he encountered in his earthly ministry. "The sufferings of this present time are not worth comparing with the glory that is to be revealed to us" (Rom. 8:18). He wraps up 2 Corinthians 4 with that very same idea:

> Though our outer self is wasting away, our inner self is being renewed day by day. For this light momentary affliction is preparing for us an eternal weight of glory beyond all comparison, as we look not to the things that are seen but to the things that are unseen. For the things that are seen are transient, but the things that are unseen are eternal. (vv. 16–18)

In view of the astounding and all-glorious reality of new-covenant gospel truth, new-covenant ministry, a mercy that flourishes in the life of an unworthy preacher under the sovereign power of God in the faithful preaching of the Word—even in the midst of being battered and bruised in the struggle—Paul embraces the perfecting power of suffering. He's faithful to his convictions. He faces life or death in the confident assurance of resurrection. And he does it all because he looks for an eternal weight of glory.

As we noted in the introduction, no one pinned a medal on Paul's chest before he departed this earth. That would have meant nothing to Paul anyway. He was looking for a reward that would come from the hand of his Savior. He told Timothy, "There is laid up for me the crown of righteousness, which the Lord, the righteous judge, will award to me on that day" (2 Tim. 4:8). He hoped to hear from the Lord, "Well done, good and faithful servant," and receive from his hand an "eternal weight of glory beyond all comparison" (2 Cor. 4:17).

The glory that phrase refers to is the glory of perfect Christlikeness. Scripture says God is even now conforming all true believers to the likeness of his Son (Rom. 8:29)—thus unveiling the glory of Christ in us. This is the same glory Paul described in 2 Corinthians 3:18: "We all, with unveiled face, beholding the glory of the Lord, are being transformed into the same image from one degree of glory to another." That describes a gradual process of transformation whereby we partake of Christ's glory in ever-increasing degrees. The word translated "transformed" in 2 Corinthians 3:18 is the same word rendered "transfigured" in Matthew 17:2, which describes how Jesus unveiled his glory on the Mount: "He was transfigured before them, and his face shone like the sun, and his clothes became white as light." The word describes a change that wholly transforms a person's being from the inside out.

On the Mount of Transfiguration Jesus had a shining face— but not like Moses's face when he came down from Sinai. The source of Jesus's glow was from within. It was much more than a transient shining that would fade as time went by; it was a reflection of the glory resident in his being, the unveiling of what he was really like, and a revelation of the true glory that was his, which he had shared with the Father from the beginning (cf. John 17:5).

We will share that glory as well. It is of course *God's* glory; it doesn't belong to us or originate with us. But because Christ indwells us, and we are being conformed to his likeness, his glory will shine through us in all its perfection. That's what Paul meant in Colossians 1:27, when he prayed that God would make known the riches of the glory of this mystery among the Gentiles, "which is *Christ in you, the hope of glory.*" It's what he had in mind in Ephesians 1:18, when he spoke of "the riches of his glorious inheritance in the saints." It should be the cherished hope of every true believer. After all, we each have "access by faith into this grace in which we stand, and we rejoice in hope of the glory of God" (Rom. 5:2).

The transformation from glory to glory may seem slow, and sometimes we might wonder if it has stalled, but the process of our sanctification will fully and instantaneously be brought to completion when at last we meet our Savior face-to-face. "We are God's children now, and what we will be has not yet appeared; but we know that when he appears we shall be like him, because we shall see him as he is" (1 John 3:2). That final, instantaneous completion of God's work in us is called "glorification" precisely because it will bring us eternally into the full light of God's glorious radiance.

That is the promise of glory Paul refers to at the end of 2 Corinthians 3 and again at the end of chapter 4. And that hope is what kept him pressing on "toward the goal for the prize of the upward call of God in Christ Jesus" (Phil. 3:14).

The ultimate "prize" is Christ himself, including a share in the riches of his glory.

Therefore we will not lose heart; we will not defect; we will not give in to evil if we live by those convictions. We will one day stand in glory, having been faithful to the end, and hear the Lord say, "Well done."

General Index

Scripture Index